Times
are
CHANGING

KARIN and KARSTEN BIE JENSEN

Archway Publishing books may be ordered through booksellers or by contacting:

Archway Publishing
1663 Liberty Drive
Bloomington, IN 47403
www.archwaypublishing.com
844-669-3957

Because of the dynamic nature of the Internet, any web addresses or links contained in this book may have changed since publication and may no longer be valid. The views expressed in this work are solely those of the author and do not necessarily reflect the views of the publisher, and the publisher hereby disclaims any responsibility for them.

Any people depicted in stock imagery provided by Getty Images are models, and such images are being used for illustrative purposes only.
Certain stock imagery © Getty Images.

Interior Image Credit: Karsten Bie Jensen, Nikolaj Olesen, Dreamstime

ISBN: 978-1-6657-2963-5 (sc)
ISBN: 978-1-6657-2964-2 (hc)
ISBN: 978-1-6657-2965-9 (e)

Library of Congress Control Number: 2022916707

Print information available on the last page.

Archway Publishing rev. date: 10/26/2022

Contents

Preface

The current theme on earth is *change*.

 This book is about these changes seen from a spiritual perspective and the larger scale of evolution, but very interestingly, also from the perspective of everyday life.

 What is going on? Why is it happening? What is the purpose? What do we need to do as individuals, if anything?

 It is also about life after death. The soul levels. Changing of genders. Values and habits here on earth, and so much more.

 This information has been given to Karin by high spiritual sources. These sources are light, intelligence, power, and speed connected with evolution on earth. We are talking very large scale.

 They are in charge of taking earth and mankind to the next level of enlightenment.

 Karin has been a channel for these light sources since she was thirty-six years old. (She's now seventy-two.)

Enjoy.

Karsten Bie Jensen

Introduction

To start writing this book has taken quite some time, years, in fact. But once I got started, it was finished in a day and a half.

Timing is a factor we respect very much.

" Karin's spiritually dictated writings. November 2021
Photo by Karsten Bie Jensen"

Knowledge has been given to me through spiritual channeling for many years (pen on paper). At times, I've received huge amounts of knowledge—about private matters, the nonphysical world, and life on earth.

Furthermore, I have used the channeling to do spiritual guiding for others. Along with my husband, Karsten, I have shown that this form of guidance can be used in different ways. Normally, when doing guidance, I write down about the person. (This is channeled information in writing.)

Karsten then explains or interprets if this is necessary. This is done online. Here's an example: A person who had been an alcoholic his whole adult life was given a spiritual guidance by his son as a present. After we performed the guiding session, the father stopped drinking. Only at special festive moments did he have a drink or two, just as advised.

This is quite a while ago. The last time we spoke to the son, his father still wasn't drinking. We're happy to pass on this type of energy work.

Cleaning Up

The time has come when I explain situations and circumstances in my life. I've had this story inside of me for twenty-three years. I have received this knowledge through communication with spiritual light/intelligence for many years. These writings have filled me with knowledge that people don't normally have access to. The information is about life on earth and in the nonphysical world, which is interesting.

What really happens when we die? What do we do? Will we come back to earth? And so much more.

In fact, this information has been given to me over long periods by these spiritual lights. The universe has lots of lights, which are knowledge, intelligence, and power on many different levels.

"The Big Dipper is part of the constellation Ursa Major, Great Bear.
There are powers in the universe beyond our imagination, connected with Earth.
Photo by Dreamstime"

This is not something I had been looking for or aimed to do. It came naturally, step by step. Personally, I have been more interested in keeping my feet on the ground by dealing with family and different types of hands-on work. To me, it's important that this type of knowledge can be used in real life.

Without a doubt, there will appear new circumstances on earth because of the light we know as the "25 Light," which is the spiritual authority of the new era on earth that lasts for approximately two thousand years. (It is what was being referred to earlier as large light sources.)

The new part in this is that the 25 Light now has access to monitor and guide people on earth and to decide and implement new values, rules to live by, and so on.

More people will see life as it *is* and start to see several aspects of life more clearly. It will be more obvious what is what and who is who.

That you change direction from time to time and that you see things from a different perspective is only natural. You become full, so to speak, when you get enough of something (in life) and remove what is no longer needed. This process is well known by most people. The difference between the past and now is speed. Speed and light will manage to implement conditions on earth as they were meant to be, for example, in areas like distribution of wealth and that the right people are in power.

People will change direction to participate in this work.

Moving forward is good. Not everyone is alike. There are different paths. There is not just *one* way in life.

Energies are multifaceted. The universe has a lot of energies and diversity, more than we know and are able to comprehend. The influence here on earth from the universe is far greater than we realize. A larger intelligence is participating than any of us have the capacity to understand.

The light will always conquer the darkness, no matter how dark it may look. That's the way the system works. The darkness is. The light is. The light always prevails over the darkness. Darkness is being implemented and enhanced from time to time on earth by the light sources.

This means that complications in daily life on all levels and situations must be dealt with and solved.

Just as we know from the laws of physics, resistance creates extra light.

The universe is made of components that we know and use here on earth—chemistry, physics, mathematics, symbols, and languages. Everything we have here is available in the universe. But we only have a small fraction of what's available out there.

We can deal with what's available here.

Distance from here to parts of outer space is being minimized. The earth's outer circumference has been expanded and is, therefore, closer to light. More about that later.

A new type of growth has arrived, and a new level of enlightenment has been inserted.

It will be implemented and unfold over a long period of time.

The cleanup is about, but not limited to, the right people being in the right place in society, distributing physical means and knowledge for the benefit of all. It's a long and complex process. We have only seen the beginning.

Recordings of Active Light

Earth has at all times been monitored by light. Previously, the light was very dim, and earth was in the dark. Life evolved in the dark. (This is seen from a spiritual and evolutionary level.) The dark protects and can be quite peaceful. It can also be wild, ferocious, and unpleasant.

Through many ages, earth has become more and more light. However, it is only *now*, during this change, that earth will be upgraded to become a light planet.

This *change of ages is happening* and is an ongoing process. The previous light, known as "15," is now slowly moving away, going to other places. It is being replaced by the light known as the 25 Light, which is much more powerful.

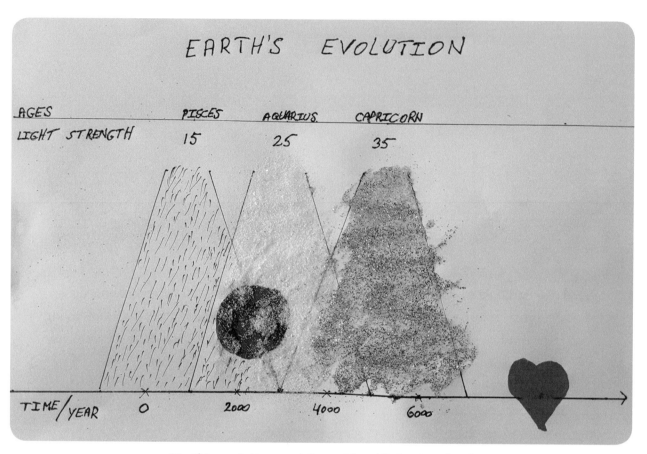

"Earth's evolution and the spiritual lights involved
By Karsten Bie Jensen"

For a long period, the 25 Light has collaborated with the 15 Light to integrate new values, rules, and agendas without being too overwhelming.

Changes have been going on for a long time. At first, nicely and quietly. People had a chance to see what was going on and to make changes willingly. Now the process is more rapid.

Examples of changes are #Metoo, changes of gender, technical areas, and communication.

Things are being seen and dealt with now because it's possible, and the time is right. Normally, every new age takes approximately two thousand years.

On the individual level, one behaves as usual. All of a sudden, habits and normal behavior just doesn't work anymore.

Earth is lit by "25." People see how unpleasant and outdated certain things are, and they must act or change.

Lots of cheating, people taking possessions that are not theirs, bad behavior, ignorance, insufficient knowledge, bad speech, and so on is being spotlighted and magnified. It can easily be detected. Every stone is being tossed and turned and later removed. This results in a better environment for everyone. These changes are only for the better.

The untouchables are being removed.

This refers to powerful people who, for years, have been able to engage in criminal activities because they were able to pay for protection.

Plenty of people with bad behavior who fear the light of day are being removed.

Things that were possible to get away with just a short while ago are no longer an option.

Lies, protection of allies with doubtful intentions, and so on are being looked at closely.

The powerful 25 Light is far more efficient and speedier than the 15 Light. Enough is enough.

One of the 25 Light's main goals is peace. Peace can never happen with all these types of cruel egos and embarrassing greed.

There's plenty for everyone. This doesn't mean that everyone should have or possess the same but that the lower levels in society will be lifted up in order to get a far better and more humane life.

There are terrible examples of how money that should have been used for a particular cause has ended up in the wrong pockets.

People were able to steal and rob. This was normal.

The dim 15 Light was not able to shine strong enough to prevent this. You can compare it to dim light in a room where you don't see things clearly.

The 25 Light requires decency, transparency, and openness. It will take time. But the process has started. The 25 Light doesn't want change to happen too fast. It would be chaotic. That is not the plan. It's a very particular exchange of all things that need an upgrade.

It's only for the better. Naturally, it will take some time. There are exact priorities about what is being highlighted and what is being changed.

Certain areas of life are outdated. They are not compatible with the new agenda in the new age. Various types of education are good examples of the speedy changes. Knowledge is accessible on a whole different level, and old authorities must redefine themselves or leave the scene.

But remember: not all that must go can be replaced at once. Some things remain for some time. Otherwise, the change would happen too fast.

Peace and quiet will take place.

Now, several different areas in life are being revealed. Politics are going to change, for example. Politicians can no longer maintain their usual pattern. The situation is difficult for many people. Changes happen, both large and small.

Communication, in general, has culminated, bursting into something quite negative. It is still possible for people who do not take part openly and with no good intentions, to express themselves *very* unpleasantly.

As soon as 25 Light is shed on communication of this kind, it will change. When you have to verify your identity to participate, this type of bad behavior will not take place any longer.

Dark places of life will be illuminated, one by one, in a very specific order. Thereby, mankind and earth get an upgrade.

Expansion of earth's outer circumference is the one absolutely most important thing in the new era.

Approximately, one-eighteenth of the earth's size has been expanded by light. This has been enabled by spiritual authorities

This gigantic work enables stages of life that were previously happening in the spirit world to take place on earth.

When we arrive here on earth, we are part of life. That, we know. Now it's possible to arrive to a stage that was previously unseen from the physical world.

Having included that part into earth's outer circumference, many more circumstances in life previously unseen will emerge as ideas and innovation physically here on earth.

It's a new dimension, a new reality. Things will occur and unfold, one by one.

People on the soul level have different genders, which is opposite male and female and also mixes of those two.

Some areas in which the soul has traveled are now part of the physical world. Previously those experiences took place in the spirit world. They have now been included as common life here on earth.

Regarding gender: the soul changes gender on the way to earth. Because of the new sphere that has been lit, we will see new gender identities. It's going to be normal. It *is* normal. Now, also in physical life. The new gender identities here on earth have come to stay. They add a little extra dimension and color to life. That's all.

We have all been through these gender changes on the way to earth, some time or another. Therefore, sooner or later, it will probably be understood.

Remember: so many things *are*. Now is the time for us to see small fractions of what is *really* available. This gives us extra useful potential here on earth for the benefit of mankind. For example in areas of technical progress and advances. We have only seen the beginning.

The volume and speed by which the technological developments are going to take place will increase noticeably. This process will help make life more pleasant for people as a whole.

This is, among other things, what the new era is about. The new possibilities will occur in due time.

Someday, all the turmoil about color, religion, gender, and so on will cease to exist. Instead, the phenomenon *accept* will occur, the word above all other words.

Accept doesn't mean that you have to participate in everything or understand everything. It means that you're not the one, who decides what is what and who does what. *You* are. *They* are. As simple as that. If there is something you don't like, just turn your focus.

There is so much of everything, more than enough. You should easily be able to find something to match your preferences. Try to leave the rest alone. It is *not* your job to play the ignorant part. Live *your* life with the possibilities that you have been given. Be sure not to be too opinionated. You don't know it all, and it's not expected that you do. Easy.

Physical Life

When you arrive on earth, your coming and going has been described by nonphysical authorities.

Several elements in your life have been decided and are going to happen. Free will is incorporated into some places where it can create better circumstances.

"New day. New Beginning. Cycles of life.
Photo by Nikolaj Olesen"

Until recently, the earth was in darkness. (It's an evolution stage.) So, if you weren't aware and alert, your light and values could be taken away by others when you (as a soul/light) traveled toward earth.

Each soul brings back light to the earth. The light itself is valuable, at times, *very* valuable. In this context, a larger light is the most valuable. *It is the result of a giant work in the nonphysical world.*

Due to the darkness associated with earth and its outer circumference, light and values could be stolen from the soul on its way to earth, by souls less powerful, only for their own benefit.

As a consequence, light, money, and values, in general, could end up in the wrong hands here on earth. It got very chaotic because those who robbed these values did not have the capacity to administer and manage money of that caliber. To manage large amounts of light and its connected values requires the proper knowledge and the right experience.

Souls and their connected light arrive here on earth to merge with the physical body. Usually, that happens just around birth. The soul has been visiting from time to time before entering and joining the body. It joins and participates as light. Parts of the soul's light are then transformed into colors at arrival. The colors are distributed in the body's chakras.

Whatever memory remains from spirit life will gradually be erased during the first time on earth.

Slowly and steadily, the child will get used to physical appearance.

From each time this process goes on, the soul's light grows and gets more experience and insight. The soul's light will always incarnate into new bodies and let some of the light transform into colors.

The extra light addition to earth's circumference has been made possible by collaboration between spiritual authorities.

Everyone who has arrived on earth for approximately the past eleven years still has whatever light they accumulated in the nonphysical world.

After a long time of fighting over values here on earth, physical values will now be distributed the way they should have.

Of course, it's a process. Those who stole possessions were greedy and selfish people who did not care about society. It was only possible because the 15 Light wasn't strong enough to prevent it.

The 25 Light will remove physical goods and possibilities in life that were stolen. These values will then be distributed rightly.

Without a doubt, many people will stand in shock because they lose physical possessions and possibly status.

This payback process has already started. That way belongings, values, and possessions will reach the proper owners. They will receive their harvests the way they should have.

"Fruits of life. Try not to take anything for granted. To feel fortunate is uplifting.
Photo by Karsten Bie Jensen"

Agreements have been made. Things and phenomena that need to be removed are often overmatched by similar phenomena, only much larger and more powerful. That way, if you don't react and remove what needs to be removed, it will feel extremely uncomfortable. This process will accelerate until you let go.

This is the background knowledge for the way many changes happen in large and small, especially when things, people, values, and so on need to be removed.

This process will arrive and eliminate parts of life that no longer belong. Others will receive the amount (in a specific order) that is going to make a difference here on earth.

To be in balance, the right size, the right circumstances, and the right possessions need to correlate.

Who are you? What are your circumstances? What are you surrounded by? These questions and issues refer to the process that will sort out and evaluate peoples' positions in society along with their status, wealth, and range of power, in large and small.

This process will happen and create peace. Too much or too little of anything causes imbalance and discomfort. All in all, it cannot be managed.

Affinity

Equal attracts equal. You only attract what you contain. You can work with your own affinity at any time if things start to go in circles without any type of comfort. Be sure that if you keep doing the same, you get the same results and experiences.

Therefore, make changes if you wish changes.

Moving around in different levels of life is good. To exchange and change habits, lifestyles, and the like is good. *You* can decide. Take action.

When you do, you'll see that new roads open and new possibilities in life occur. In order to do this, you must not be tangled up in old habits without any *real* presence and value.

Sometimes life will help present new ideas.

Catch the ideas that are useful in areas that make a difference, areas for new thoughts, emotions, and actions. Catch them, embrace them, and get to know them.

The word *accept* is magnificent.

Expand your circles. A fresh start gives you a chance to minimize too much self-assurance. Enhance respect for other peoples' areas in life.

To dare participate with your vulnerability, as if you were a rookie, can be positive at times.

Finding out what you don't want, or are ready for, is just as important. Being able to say a clear *yes* or a clear *no* can be very useful.

Taking a new route or trying something entirely new will always seem like a journey where you get a new life experience. The more you travel, the faster you know how to adapt and which way to choose.

Tune in on what's important and leave the little things alone. Sometimes it's a good idea to set things into perspective. That way, you don't misjudge tiny little things and make them seem like important matters.

Making the wrong choices can create a sense of unease and make you feel distracted.

To take it easy.

To wait, to *see* is important. Not always top speed from the beginning.

Steadily learn to read the language of life that shows you new territories.

"The tree of life. Rooted, tranquil -
experienced, in harmony. Fresh air and plenty of space.
More to gain, more to give. Peace.
Photo by Karsten Bie Jensen"

Distance is an important part when changing affinity. It helps when old habits are out of reach.

Many people are afraid of changes in life. That's a shame. Changes can give the necessary alertness and a sense of presence, which is of great benefit not only for oneself but also for mankind's opportunities for coexistence.

This does not mean we all have to be in the same boat at once. There are differences.

If the differences are too big, it's not possible to coexist. There must be some type of border or boundary. Not for everybody else, but for you!

This is a self-imposed boundary or protection. One should stop wasting energy on matters of little importance and learn to prioritize.

On the other hand, try not to get involved in areas of life where you don't interact or belong, by expressing your thoughts and opinions.

If you don't respect that, you become part of the "game," and you will not be able to attract what is yours.

Be in the right environment where you fit in. Expand whenever your own understanding, and experience grows. It's about timing.

At any given time, it's good to leave environments you no longer feel affiliated with.

Many people will experience that their growth is held back or maybe even impossible due to certain people's presence. These people do not respect the growth of others but try to cling on to or put down those who seek growth.

Protect yourself against others who try to interfere in your life. Life is too important to let anyone participate when they shouldn't.

Protect the presence of people in your surroundings and the lifestyle that suits you.

This means that however different you may be, you should respect other people's choices, paths, and life journeys fully.

Don't let anybody else interfere with your life without your agreement. Have no doubt that no one has the right to do so. *No one.*

Bies Diet

Bies Diet is food being used as medicine. It is individually prescribed.

Karsten and I have developed the Bies Diet plan concept over a period of thirty years, on and off.

The beginning was very slow and required a lot of work—daily phone calls with clients. At that time, the foods were *plus*, *minus*, and *neutral*. I kept records and made journals. Hundreds of food items were involved. There were changes every day. All sorts of produce, different foods, and beverages were tested, and whether biodynamic, organic, or conventionally produced items made a difference. Fresh, frozen, canned, freeze-dried, and so on were tested. In the Bies Diet system, there is no difference in the result whether you choose a fresh biodynamic, organic, or conventionally grown corn, or if you choose frozen, canned, or freeze-dried corn. All these types have the same effect for the user.

You may have an opinion about which quality you prefer, and that's fine. Please feel free to choose the one that suits you best.

After many years of constantly developing Bies Diet, we find that the current form has reached a level that is super easy and convenient for the user.

When you order a diet plan, you will receive a list with four to eight different items of produce. There may also be a beverage included. It's an individually made plan. The person does not need to be present. It's been like that for thirty-six years. We work through energies, and we need very little information about the client.

The diet plan is plant-based. You only have to eat the foods once daily. (The same goes for the beverage, if that's part of the plan.) Every item must be consumed by what equals a teaspoonful. It's not a complete change of diet but food as medicine, as previously mentioned, four to eight teaspoonfuls daily for two months.

Eat what you normally do. There's nothing you can't eat unless you're allergic or have some kind of intolerance. There is a questionnaire regarding these issues in the ordering process on the website.

Many costumers have experienced changing their normal diets after having started Bies Diet. But that's a whole different story. It's nothing that we're involved in or recommend.

Our experiences through the years have included several ailments, among those are *migraines, stomach problems, ear drainage, insomnia,* and *menopause.*

I have used food as medicine for more than three decades.

An ear specialist who saw Bies Diet work openly declared that food had nothing to do with the healing. That was the general attitude back then.

What happened was an exchange of energy, so big that one expert after another expressed their feelings and beliefs about diet and health. Some of them only had very limited experience regarding nutrition-related health. Others had much more knowledge and wanted to participate. A new trend was starting.

It was difficult to focus because of all the noise, excitement, opinions, and such going on.

Of course, another thing is timing, which is a very important factor.

That food has a big impact on human health, along many other factors, is ancient knowledge. Medicine back then was based on several things, among other herbs in the monasteries, the natural medicines, and the use of yin and yang energies in food as well as knowledge about macrobiotic. Nothing new there.

Nutrition, along with other things, are extremely interesting when it comes to health.

That people are very much alike and at the same time, extremely different is well known. That food as medicine is individual, like in Bies Diet, is probably less known. It's been like that during all the thirty-six years I've worked with food as medicine. Always individually.

At first, I used a pendulum to measure the energies. Through the years, we have continued developing the program and formula. At times, we have worked with people being present. At other times, they were not. Currently, we only work without the client being present. It's possible to order a Bies Diet plan from all over the world through online contact. Bies Diet is based in Henderson, Nevada, United States.

For more information about Bies Diet: *www.biesdiet.com*

No one had thought this possible, being able to heal several physical ailments and mental conditions. Bies Diet is energy work of very high caliber. Behind this idea, there is a huge background and experience through unity of physical and nonphysical incarnations.

Try not to understand more than this. To exercise this trade has given a very large insight about exactly how big an influence the nonphysical world has on earth.

Energies of great speed and power participate to remove the ailments. It is not generally known that spiritual energies can perform at such a level.

Very large and powerful energies can participate and work continuously through the right channels. These channels have worked physically and nonphysically. Both the physical and nonphysical participations are required to connect these worlds.

"Taurus relates to values, in astrology.
Physically and spiritually. Photo by Dreamstime"

Having access to energies of that magnitude ensures that the channeling of energies happens promptly, accurately, and safely. This line of business requires many, many incarnations of hard work—physically and nonphysically. To be a channel for these powerful energies requires focus on what is essential and leaving the rest alone, finding essence and sticking to that. It requires utmost peace and being undisturbed.

I have performed this type of work for thirty-six years.

So much has happened.

Natural elements along with the influence of the most powerful lights/energies have created tremendous results.

Many of our clients had tried conventional medical treatment with little or no success.

An example was a mother who brought her son. He had previously been treated by Bies Diet for using ear drainage, and was healed. Now he had a stomach problem that the doctors weren't sure how to diagnose. But it was decided that the boy needed surgery. The mother was in a state of despair when she remembered how Bies Diet had helped her son some years back. Again, Bies Diet was able to help the boy. He was healed and subsequently didn't have to get surgery.

Ineffective elements have been used for too long. These expensive circumstances must be improved soon and participate in finding new ways of collaborating and exercising treatment. (This means that people who work for their own benefit, are wasting time and resources meant for the good of all).

Several of my clients were sent by the local hospital, where they were positive toward my kind of business.

Why not keep focus on the important healing part. That would leave room for a very beneficial collaboration. This is not impossible. I've done it before. I suggest and recommend that this type of work is focused on result and collaboration, not who did what—or how, and why.

Bies Diet

The World of Emotions

The world of emotions, also called the astral world, is undergoing change.

Old, worn-out emotions must go. It is a general state of evolution but dealt with individually.

A way of expressing the current condition: the world of emotions has become like unclear waters.

Many people are ready for new emotional input.

The current change of ages is going to implement new emotional values. Old elements from this world will be exchanged. This change and exchange will take place all over the world. This is going to happen in several ways and at different levels to assure that people are more fit and capable of contributing positively.

New areas and possibilities flourish. This means that the heart chakra must open for most people. This will happen through circumstances in life. It is not something the individual person can decide to do or not. It will be controlled, directed, and implemented by the 25 Light in due time.

The pure-hearted, clean emotions must open now to benefit everyone.

To be is the essence.

This is done by people who work selflessly for the benefit of society. People with no greed or wish to be seen for their own purpose.

"New water, crystal clear.
Symbolizes filtered emotions and new start.
Photo by Nikolaj Olesen"

Try to ease your emotions.

Protect yourself from wanting something that doesn't work any longer.

Let go.

Move away from rock-solid parts of life that are unable to be part of the change.

Don't plan too far ahead.

In new times, there is always change involved. This is a process that is necessary.

Take little steps that seem obvious. Start listening to your purest emotions. That is where *real* knowledge is.

Be in the right environments, which are often peaceful, less outgoing, slower.

Get some peace and quiet to see what's really going on. Be aware and be sure that if things you try fail, you can just let them go. On the other hand, receive things in life that are shown you and given you more effortlessly.

People are different and on different paths. In some areas of life, we are alike.

Others, not so much. Be aware that life is moving forward. Do not focus emotionally on what happened earlier.

To study what happened and keep digging in the past does not make sense. It is often a shadow world that has been outlived. Focus on the present and the road leading forward away from the more emotional world. If it keeps clinging on to you, try to let go.

Give it as little energy as possible. It's easier if you focus on going forward. Let light work for you and what is happening now.

It's a journey, a road. If you are worn out from time to time, take a rest. Then continue your work. Don't despair if you feel overwhelmed by the past. That's natural

Prioritize how you spend your time. Say no and let go if you don't feel in harmony with what's going on. This could be related to anything from the past.

Everything has a time. Everything has a start.

In every major change, speech is important. Don't talk about things you find negative. Ignore them. Focus on something different. Let positivity fill your day as much as possible, also, in the way you speak.

When you choose to take part in verbal battle zones, you participate no matter what you say. Therefore, stay away. Very meticulously choose where you participate.

Most issues can be viewed upon from so many sides anyway. If you must say something, choose the right place and time. It's more simple and easier not to participate. Let it go, by not commenting.

Remain focused. It is always possible to find something of positive nature in your life.

We're not talking about if or when you're going through great grief, for any reason. This is human. Give yourself time. Work through your sorrow the best way you can.

The kind of positivity we're talking about is in everyday life, the days that are common for most people. To focus on positivity, to address someone positively. Stay calm and use friendliness.

It's important to use friendliness in society in general.

Don't be too busy.

Nature can be a good help for many. Just stay in the calm.

Woods, parks, and the like can all be good environments in this process of balancing your emotions.

Remember that *you* choose in your life, what you look at, what you listen to, who you spend time with. Choose what is best for you.

Do you lack time? Try to turn off the TV. That way it's easier to stay focused on what's going on in your life.

A change is ready. You can contribute by making more deliberate choices. It may be difficult at first. But through wanting it enough, it will be easier after some time. Take little steps. Look at the response you get and evaluate.

Learn to read the language of life.

Maybe you feel harmony and like where you are in life. Maybe you are good at making the right choices. Then obviously, you don't need to change anything. It's only if you experience that things do *not* work.

Show who you are. You have a right to be you because you're here. Maybe your influence could be positive in areas you are not aware of.

Quite often, we don't see ourselves clearly. Now and again, we may wonder why somebody else thinks that something we did was absolutely fantastic. We may not think it was anything at all. Things we do almost effortlessly, we hardly notice, because they're as easy as brushing our teeth.

Please remember: when something is very easy, it is only because you have worked in this particular area in the nonphysical world as well as in the physical, through several incarnations.

This expertise does not come out of the blue. It's not a coincidence. It's the result of many incarnations. It's an ability you have inside of you.

The soul, or your soul light, has enormous resources in areas where you have worked/practiced and feel comfortable.

Some people may say that it is so easy for you doing this specific thing. Maybe it's true. But you have worked hard for it. Remember that.

On the other hand, you may not understand that at times, when you try really hard, no one notices. It's because you are learning, and the result of your work is probably not very noticeable.

Many people have large amounts of light, experience, knowledge, and talent within.

However, and unfortunately, not everyone gets a chance to use his or her talents, even if they are far superior to any education available.

Many people are influenced by other people's expectations, norms, and traditions. That's obvious.

In many countries people are being overeducated. It's because there is more status to taking a seven-year-long university degree than staying true to yourself and using your talents within.

In fact, in some cases, the light, knowledge, and experience you have within may be turned off because you're trying to live up to other people's expectations. That's a shame.

This is not mentioned to put down education or educational systems. It's just a reminder that some people have what they need in life regarding knowledge and expertise inside of them. They are born with it. In those cases, what these people need is support to find their own ways in life more than anything.

I mention this only to cast a light on these types of people because their expertise is very valuable and should be treasured and accepted. If you belong to this group who has this inner knowledge and expertise, you should try to believe in yourself and find your own way. It is not less valuable being self-taught, if that is what you choose. Quite the opposite.

Let's try to accept that there are many more types of intelligence than we understand and appreciate currently.

Again, nothing negative about the educational systems. A broader understanding of the term *knowledge* is what is useful.

Life on Soul Level

As we leave the physical world, the soul (light) leaves the body and moves toward the soul level: the nonphysical world. There, in the heavens, the soul will take part in places where it belongs, as far as it has developed.

Rarely do we get all our soul light with us when we incarnate on earth. We get the amount of light that is suitable for our lives and tasks here on earth, for each time. This means that when our soul light leaves our physical body when we die, it will travel back to where it came from and reunite with the remaining light. Then the soul light leaving the body, plus the remaining light in the soul level, will gather and be ready for further development as *one*.

A very deep sleep occurs. That way the soul forgets about life on earth.

There are *very* deep sleeps involved with changes from physical to nonphysical life and vice versa. This type of deep sleep removes whatever memory that may remain. Usually, this is a calm and slow process. It ensures that the soul, whether on the soul level or incarnated on earth, can focus on the current life chapter. If we remembered all incarnations and nonphysical lives, it would be too confusing. The experience, knowledge, and skills are layered in the soul for each incarnation and soul life.

The soul is granted whatever skills and knowledge are required for each incarnation. This knowledge will unfold throughout life in due time, if needed.

At the soul level, there are usually work tasks to perform. This is where the soul *really* develops. This is where the soul collects knowledge and insight.

On the soul level, there are both female and male souls, plus, several mixes of the two. There are many divisions, departments, and levels in the soul world. Families exist, friends exist, more types of souls than we are aware of.

Usually, a male soul has many powerful tasks to perform. A male soul will solve lots of assignments if it works hard enough. Therefore, it needs a little rest later on. A male soul usually incarnates into a female body on earth. Previously, in some cultures, and per definition, women could live a more relaxed type of lifestyle, not so pushy and extroverted.

Many women are extremely strong, stronger than most men if they use their inner soul's power. They can easily overrule the man if that's what they want.

For female souls, it's the opposite. The female soul usually incarnates into a male body on earth. It balances the understanding and energy of male/female life and development.

Most men are more vulnerable than women. To compensate for that, masculinity can be used.

It's on the soul level that actual development takes place. When returning to the soul world, the soul will get an overview of the past life on earth in addition to explanations about what just happened in that life. We are shown episodes from life, areas where we now can work and develop. Soon thereafter, we start different tasks meant for us.

We meet our real families here. Some of us have incarnated on earth together. Others not.

Some have had assignments in the dark, here on earth, in order for larger light sources to be able to enter that area. This doesn't mean that those leading the way belong there. But that larger light sources can follow when another light (humans) show the way.

Obviously, it can be unpleasant to see how mankind behaves in the dark. But certain very highly developed souls know, at a given point in time, why they were placed in the darkness of earth. This refers to the time before the 25 Light became the main authority on earth.

Now there's enough light on earth for the 25 Light to monitor and register what's going on and why. That's why things can be changed.

***

Lots of worlds exist on the soul level. This is where your life is, basically.

On the soul level, souls don't recognize each other the way we do on earth, and they have no memory of their physical incarnations. That memory disappears.

When returning to soul life, there's a thorough explanation about what just happened in earth life, then the sleep. The explanation is layered in the soul, like other experiences, but is not part of the memory/conciseness. You can compare it to something that happened earlier in your life that you have forgotten. It is still part of your experience, even if you don't remember it.

Souls recognize each other via vibrations, energy, and light.

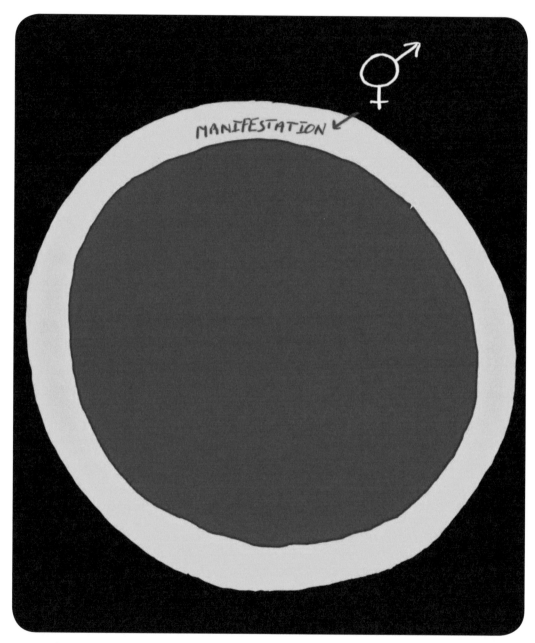

"Earth's outer circumference where new types of manifestation can take place"

Because an extra layer of light has been added around the earth, people will start experiencing other energies at certain times in life. Currently, some people are quite lonely because of the pandemic, which is obvious. Many get to know inner feelings and sides of their personalities they were not aware of. It may be overwhelming.

In fact, sometimes a short break is necessary. If so, take a rest.

All you need is food and rest and few people around you—that's all. Then after a while, you'll be ready to participate in life again.

Should this occur to you, make sure you get enough time on your own and that somebody will help take care of the necessities. Make everything ultra-easy, precooked foods and the like. Everything should be as convenient as possible.

Downsize. Focus and prioritize on peace and quiet. Know that you don't necessarily need medicines or anything else. Stay in the peace, which is actually a gift. You should take care of yourself the best way possible. Enjoy just *to be* for a moment. Then start fresh again. It's an important way to get a break. You will be fine.

Spiritual Add-Ons

A way to explain spiritual add-ons is: the more you exercise any given ability in life, the better you become and the more strength you have. In certain areas, the add-ons can manifest from the spirit world. When you have used your own willpower long enough, you will see, if it is positively, that things can go super smoothly. Sometimes you only need to be present, then most everything will succeed.

A nonphysical power and energy can be added in areas where you work really hard. However, this system is two-sided, meaning that if you work on negative issues, negative forces will be added to your project or your personality, or both. (Negativity in this context can be corruption, self-empowerment, violent actions, and the like.) And this will affect you negatively. Both positivity and negativity can accelerate that way.

Be aware of your actions. If you know you're doing something that you really shouldn't, then don't. As easy as that. Just stop.

If you're doing something wrong in an area that you're not aware of, you cannot fix it. There are many things we're not aware of. It's when we know that it counts.

A good guideline is to try to implement light yourself, to see if what you do is something that you will show or share with others. You can practice and get very far that way by being honest to yourself. That way you can clean up in areas that you're aware of. Just like training physically, you can practice habits, speech, and so on.

On the largest scale, huge light sources are also being added. Every age, which is approximately two thousand years, has a new light, which is the power in control. The light connected with the age that is finishing was known as the 15 Light source. In that light, there was still more dark than light on earth. But with the new 25 Light, earth is being lit. *Many* energy/light add-ons are being implemented. These huge lights do not fight to be in control. Every light has its era with new plans, rules, and agendas.

By the time the 15 Light had been here for approximately a thousand years, the 25 Light slowly started to participate. When 15 Light needed help, or doubted what to do, it could ask for help by the 25 Light. It has a larger knowledge, insight, power, monitoring ability, speed, and so on.

During the last thousand years 15 Light was in charge, 25 Light participated and helped, - slowly, slowly, more and more. At a given point in time, 25 Light will take over entirely.

The 25 Light will implement new agendas, rules, and ways of life on earth. For the next age, the 25 Light will work to implement peace on earth as one of the main goals. It will happen within the next two thousand years.

Currently, the 25 Light is taking over, but the 15 Light is not completely out. It's a long, gentle and timely process.

The way it works is that in approximately two thousand years, when it is time for a new age, it will be the "35 Light" that takes over control of earth.

The same process of lights helping each other is going to take place. The 25 Light will ask for help from 35 Light. This is the pattern of evolution on earth.

Currently, the 15 Light is moving out, the 25 Light taking over, and the 35 Light is on standby for the coming age, two thousand years from now. At any given time, the current light in charge can seek guidance by the next bigger light/intelligence.

How things should be managed on earth is a huge collaboration by giant light sources. It is evolution on a large scale.

Currently, there is a lot of cleaning up going on. Timing, monitoring, developing, educating, implementing and so on are main factors.

The next big step for mankind is being able to use the heart chakra, which has a lot more to offer.

For example, in business, it is more important now than ever that there is a larger goal than just making money for the owners and shareholders.

On the personal level, it's becoming trendier to give and support rather than focusing on egocentric needs.

At one point, during the next two thousand years, there will be peace on earth when things that don't belong have been removed and efforts have been made wholeheartedly with sincerity and genuine presence. People will be enriched with new spheres and possibilities.

The 25 Light's main purpose is peace. It will happen at one point. Let's hope that peace can start soon. In small areas, groups of people will get together in life.

It's a long way, two thousand years from now. But let we all who are able to look beyond our egos participate as much as possible.

It's up to each individual to determine and recognize when and in which areas of life to participate. It can be done in large and small.

The next age represented by 35 Light is much more powerful. It will be about manifestation.

It means, not so much back and forth, as we know from this era.

Let us use time wisely. Those who know and recognize that people have a right to be here in decent circumstances and under right conditions, buckle up.

The Mental World

The mental world is a world by itself, just like the emotional and the physical worlds, but with access to the other worlds. Every one of these worlds is an independent unit.

Some people are very developed in the mental world, and maybe not so developed in the emotional world. Sometimes we see highly intelligent people act totally out of control and very childish in the emotional world, and vice versa. Some people stop developing at age four (just as an example). For some reason, they get a block in the emotional level and start compensating through the mental world.

It is always possible to work in an area/world that needs development. Of course, you need to be aware of it and have insight about that particular area. Otherwise, you just feel that the given area can be really difficult to maneuver in and sense a sort of stagnation.

The mental world is superior to the emotional and physical worlds. When the mental capacity is strong enough, it will control emotions and what is important in the physical world. If there is too much imbalance and turmoil going on, it can reflect on emotions and actions in unfortunate ways.

The mental world is working overtime these days. Many people collapse or get diagnosed with stress.

It's just too much.

At the same time, the emotional world is set on standby. The reason is there's no time or energy to feel anything or act/behave with presence and creativity. Many actions, and life in general, easily become routine and robotic. For the time being, it's a good idea to leave as much as possible alone. *Prioritize* is the keyword.

There is so much information, so many things going on, big and small. Areas from all over the world are accessible. Many people are busy, too busy, because of all the input of important as well as indifferent information. Valuable genuine presence is being lost when that happens. It's like being on a slide. You lose your empathy and don't notice others or yourself properly.

Longer breaks from work are needed. Sick leaves and so on seems like the only solution. Slow speed does not exist. Full speed, with hardly any presence is the current agenda for many people.

The mental world needs peace and quiet. You need to stay in the present. Let yourself get a rest. It can be very difficult to calm down if you're driving full speed. Take on new parts in life that you really like instead of too much repeating in your head. It's not making a big difference anyway. One tends to keep certain patterns in life, which is also true for the mindset. The mind needs peace.

It is healthy to take a break from time to time from many things in life. Realize that they may not be that important altogether. Realize how small a difference many things make. Does it make any difference at all? Is it for the better? And so on.

Take good care of yourself instead. Eat some nice food, - food that *you* like. Enjoy nature, the quiet in nature. Look at something that's uplifting. Get a good massage, for example. Manage to get time for something that you really like to do. This makes you want to *be* in emotional and physical presence. You can choose between almost anything that you really like.

If, or when, you experience a time like this, you need to take care of yourself for a while. Do things that make you feel happy and content. Some of it, you have to do by yourself, of course, since it's only you who know exactly what these areas in life are that comforts and soothes you. This is *very* important.

As you well know, you cannot make a difference for anybody else if you lack energy. Potentially, it can result in unpleasant situations. Like on planes and boats when there is an emergency situation, take care of yourself first. Put on the mask, the life vest, and so on, before you help others. If you don't, everyone will be in danger.

Your thoughts need to be calm. To reach that point, you need quietness, comfort and to focus.

It's important to change habits. Think about all the knowledge that's available. Previously, people had to memorize a lot, so many things in their heads. That's not the case anymore. Now we need to make good use of the many kinds of electronic devices available, phones, tablets, laptops, and so on. It will make everything easier.

It is not very attractive that your head is overbooked. It's a misunderstanding. In the past, it was a sign of importance if you were busy and fully booked. In business and privately. That is not so much the case any longer.

Rest, tranquility, meditation, and peaceful activities with less speed and stress can all be valuable factors. To have enough time for family and self-contemplation is becoming trendy. To have empathy, to be a giving person, to be a good listener, and to have enough time and presence is now desirable. There is a clear, obvious change of values and priorities.

Ending—Start

When a life chapter ends, another one begins. That's a fact. Maybe not in the same instant but as soon as you're ready. Accept that everything is under development. Everything. Not one second is alike, worldwide. Everything that we know, live, and die. Flies, blood cells, trees, and so forth.

Everything has a time. We know that. Generally speaking, ending processes don't have our full interest or understanding. It's very good that we live in the present. Somehow, we know that all along the way there are huge changes in big and small.

The big light that is currently connected to earth makes sure that things happen a lot faster than previously. Some people have experienced that already by gaining or losing things, status, and possessions rapidly. The 25 Light source enables several circumstances in life to start and finish much faster than before.

We need to raise the bar in many areas of life here on earth. That's why things have been speeding up, for earth to become a light planet.

"To feel rooted in between changing life chapters is comforting.
Photo by Karsten Bie Jensen"

It's important to see that things happen just around us. A lot of changes, that's for sure. The 25 Light source is quite exact.

So, stay in the change that is going on. Some things in life are outdated and need to change. We can't always see it ourselves. If we could, we would have done something about it. We need to remember that the current powerful light makes us see things we didn't see before. These areas in life are going to withdraw, making room for the new. That's the essence.

Things that no longer match the new era have taken up space and need to go. Then a new chapter can begin. Yet some of the old values, mindsets, and so on are fit to be used in the new age. There is going to be an evaluation of the existing, the new, and things being removed in order to make a proper match.

Everything will be uplifted. Without any doubt. Many areas in life will vanish and be gone soon. There will be so many other things to attend to. Indifferences will be removed. Things in life that were previously very important need to go, because they don't correlate with the new world.

It's a system. That's just the way it is.

Some things in life may be put on hold while new areas take their place. Don't be afraid to put things on hold. If it's relevant for the future, it will come back in due time.

The phenomena called attraction is working constantly. Some old elements of life will need to go. They are being replaced by newer, lighter models.

This has been normal for some time. But it is going to be a different world.

Many more electronic devices are being developed for purposes that we haven't seen yet. It is a speedy process.

Thoughts and ideas will spread. Remarkable new things will occur.

New ages make a huge difference in life. Other than that, every new generation is a plus for earth. They are filled with all the new ideas, innovation, and energy useful for the new times.

That new generations see older generations as not being very useful is obvious. This is the power that pushes them forward. Remember: they're bringing all the new for the benefit of mankind. It shouldn't be a fight between generations but a common journey wherever it's possible.

Religions

Many, many roads lead to the spiritual part of life. Some choose that path. Others don't. It's of great importance to understand that everyone chooses his or her way, whatever they find suitable. There is often a cultural background behind a choice. All choices are just fine.

Many times, it's obvious how different these paths are. All the paths are usable and undergoing development.

Just as everything else, things happen for a reason.

People who brought religions were often ones who had visions or clear sights of some kind. Others then joined.

As we all know, religions have been blamed for a lot. As in all areas of life, there are good guys and bad guys. That's just the way it is. Unfortunately, darkness on earth has prevented cleaning out of the bad guys, in religions. We know that things have been going on that shouldn't have. Wrong things, sometimes in the name of God. These elements will be removed by the 25 Light.

Incompetent people have been able to rule and create awful circumstances. It's been possible because the 15 Light wasn't strong enough.

Not one religion is bad. Not one religion is good. There is good and bad all over. Whole religions, plus the whole system, will be filtered and cleaned.

The ways of religions, the rules, the laws, keep people on a spiritual track. Many old traditions remain in religions. That's fine as long as it doesn't harm anybody. No one is more right than others. It's about hope, believing, recognition, tradition, or something of great importance.

Every path has its issues. Along the way, there has been plenty of power abuse. That's obvious to most people. Like in many areas in life, there will be great development, uplifting, and cleaning in the religious spheres.

For many people, religions are important. For some, not so much. For others, it's just a dot. And for some, not even an option. Remember: the world is colorful. One should feel free to use the possibilities that seem right and important.

That religions like to fight among one another is also well known. Religions want to show and convince that *their* way is the right way or the best way. It probably is for them. But again, remember that we're different and each person chooses what is right for him or her.

Many people see religions as a whole connected group of people. That is a shame. It is overly simplified.

We have personally lived in the Maldives for eleven years. And as the only non-Muslims in our island, we have been totally included. There hasn't been one word about different religions. On the contrary, sometimes we talk to people from the local community about religions leading to the same place.

Among our closest friends are Muslims, Mormons, Catholics, atheists, Christians, and more.

Religions are fine as long as they are used by the right people. Therefore, kindly clean out fanatics. That way, peaceful elements can participate, enjoy life, and coexist.

New Water

Several parts of life and some people are going to be removed rapidly, especially those who have held on to power and authority for their own sake and benefit.

When previous authorities in life hold on to their past successes, power, and identities without giving room for new values and possibilities, it tends to get odd or tragic.

That's because the new ideas and talents can be delayed in their progress if too much attention is given the has-beens.

It can be difficult to let go, especially for those who were defining the past.

People of the new world are empathetic, listeners, collaborators, who act from the place where we must all act—the heart.

When people learn to trust and use their hearts, they will be able to embrace, give, and receive. They will also evaluate, distribute, create, and collaborate on a much higher level than before.

Due to the new 25 Light and the increased speed with which things will evolve in general, there will be little room, if any, for people who work for their own agenda and benefit.

To change these elements is not only necessary, but it's almost going to happen by itself, because of the very strong light. The closer it gets, the more obvious this becomes.

Apart from the new, powerful light, the main difference now is speed. Again and again, the experts are going to be shocked by the speed and the fact that things have already happened. It's not so strange. Time has surpassed old-fashioned calculations.

Many do a great job in investigating what is good. But as we all know, a lot of experts disagree.

There is no way that the experts can agree on something that happens so fast. It's called learning by doing.

The language of life is clear. The speed is new and difficult to handle. Thus, *calm down*. Take it easy. Take care of the little things that matter.

Start practice using your heart chakra. Know that you can feel and sense things there if you are attentive.

Notice when it feels calm, easy, and nice, and when it feels uneasy, anxious, turmoil-like. Try to change the things that give you unease.

Unease can be related to all areas of life. The uneasiness is a feeling that requires attention. It's totally individual, and from time to time, it can be a strong or not so strong feeling. It can mean getting rid of this or that thing, situation, and so on. Change focus. Stop a habit. Change friends. Acquire something, start something—there are many possibilities.

Maybe it is difficult to act on something that you *feel*. But try. Try at least in the beginning to see what happens when you make little changes. Maybe it removes the uneasiness. If that works, you will slowly become braver and learn to trust the feelings/communication in your heart.

To act from the heart is going to happen here on earth. Humanity is under constant development. The current transition from dark to light demands change.

We see it clearly, the change. It becomes more and more obvious. Know that the heart is the next big step for mankind to conquer.

It is also obvious how uncomfortable many people are despite all the physical wealth they possess. It does not make a difference when the heart chakra is left out. Then, it's about *me me* and *more more*.

There is no contact or connection to how fortunate or how privileged a lot of people are. It's like an oasis of so many fine things. Still, it seems like empty shells as long as there is no connection to the heart.

To complain about little things is common. To have anxiety and anger within, feelings that leap out, uncontrolled, is sad.

To miss physical possessions is good when they become so commonplace that we don't appreciate them anymore. When we take things for granted, they tend to lose their value. There's a good chance that we become indifferent, or even obnoxious toward those things. It's not pretty when gratitude and awareness is missing.

As in other areas in life, you can practice what makes things valuable for you. Get used to—and practice—being grateful for what you have. Be thankful for what is happening in your life and so on. If it's difficult, try to minimize what you have or what you do.

Maybe you have acquired too much. Give something away. Or just do something. Maybe there are too many activities. Choose just a few. You can do it if you want.

Of course, if your life is on track, and you feel fine, then you don't need to do anything.

Karin Bie Jensen

Epilogue

The time is *now*!

To understand just a little bit more.

To let go.

To change direction.

To participate.

To give accept.

To start using the heart in communication and navigation.

Humanity and earth are connected, not just to each other, but to huge spiritual light sources previously unknown to humankind.

In this context, "Let there be light" means "to be enlightened"!

Embrace the new knowledge. Try to understand and implement new values.

Collaborate. Be patient.

Give. Build. Nourish.

We wish to express our deepest gratitude for being able to participate in starting and implementing the new era.

Karsten Bie Jensen

LUCKY is a self-experienced travel adventure, told mainly in pictures. However, there are plenty of stories and descriptions. Positive, friendly, embracing, warm-hearted, and very colorful.

It is about passion for life and navigating via the heart.

Most of the photos are from the Maldives where Karin and Karsten live and owned a guesthouse for 10 years.

Other destinations are the US., Greenland, Sri Lanka, France, Korea, Denmark, and Bangladesh.

It's an inspiring story about meeting the World with open arms and hearts through curiosity. Combined with a genuine interest in foreign cultures, food, and uplifting moments.

Karin and Karsten are a married couple from Denmark.

The passion for food brought them together, as teacher and student.

Family, good food, music, travels, sports, arts, ocean activities, and spiritual enlightenment are their main interests.

They live in the Maldives. Until Covid 19 hit, they owned a guesthouse on the island of Velidhoo for 10 years.

Bies Diet (food as medicine) is their online business in Henderson NV. USA. Find out more at: BiesDiet.com

JENSEN

Lucky to travel • Lucky to work • Lucky to feel loved

L U C K Y
a travel autobiography

Activate your senses —
come join us in the Maldives and other exotic places.

Karsten Bie Jensen

By the same authors

Printed in the United States
by Baker & Taylor Publisher Services